Carol & ... "

To ...

who hav... ...rs.

thoughtfu... ...

I have many fond memories of our good times together.

♡ Julie ♡

When A Classmate Dies

Julie Berg

PRAIRIE HOUSE

ISBN 0-911007-21-0.
Library of Congress data on request.

First edition 1991.

Prairie House Inc.
Box 9199
Fargo, North Dakota 58106-9199

Contents

Our Special Friend, Randy

by Mrs. Berg's 2nd Grade Class

We loved Randy so much.
Randy taught us a lot about courage.
He shared his love with all of us.
He showed us a real meaning of friendship.
Randy showed us that friends are so very special. Because of Randy we have made so many new special friends.
He taught us never to give up, but to always keep trying.

He taught us that little things
mean a lot because he loved every
little note we sent him every day.
Randy cared for us and showed us
how to care for others.
We are so sad that Randy died.
We will miss Randy so much.
But yet we will never ever
forget him.
We are thankful that Randy
is at peace now.

Chapter 1

Terminally Ill Students

When a Classmate Dies is in memory of a very special teacher — Sharon Christa McAuliffe, our first "Teacher in Space."

Christa McAuliffe once said, "I always encourage my students to go beyond the limitations they have set for themselves. You know, to push themselves a little bit. You just don't know what's going to be around the next corner."

The Christa McAuliffe Fellowship made it possible for me to share with many primary students and primary teachers throughout our nation many things about life and death that our second grade class learned from a very special seven-year-old.

During the 1987–1988 school year, one of the students assigned to my second grade class was a little boy with acute non-lymonocytic leukemia. My first contact with Randy was in a hospital room prior to the start of the school year. During this first visit, I recognized his eagerness to learn; he was excited and enthusiastic as I read *Corduroy*, by Don Freeman, to him while he held my own corduroy teddybear. As a teacher I felt a responsibility to encourage his desire and to enhance the feeling that Randy was an important member of our class along with the other students.

Knowing that Randy could be terminally ill did not alter my responsibility for teaching him or for including him in as many class activities as possible. But since I had not taught a terminally ill child during my teaching career, I had some questions and wanted some guidance that would clarify my position. When I went to look for resources and references, I found limited information that would help me explain to my young class about illness and dying, or ideas and activities to help the dying child and his/her classmates.

Even though Randy spent most of his academic year at home and in hospitals working with tutors, he became an important member in our second grade class. He had much to give to his classmates and they to him. Together they experienced courage, love, sadness, happiness, caring and sharing.

To lift his spirits during this serious time of his life, each school day we sent Randy "rays of sunshine"; packages of worksheets, letters or artwork from the daily class activities. Special time was not needed to complete the activity.

After school the students took turns mailing Randy's package, an opportunity to do something for Randy, which made each child feel special. Whoever mailed the package had his/her name written on it so Randy knew who had gone to the post office that day. We learned that "little things mean a lot" because each time Randy returned to the hospital, he took all our mail along.

In classrooms today there are students of many different abilities and capabilities. Schools have varied curriculum for each child's needs and are continuing to change the curriculum to adapt to each individual child. Educators need to remember that each child is special and unique. Educators need to be sensitive and aware of each child's feelings and thoughts; they won't find answers universal for all children, but educators can provide for individual needs. Helping children cope with the illness and death of a classmate or a loved one is actually helping children to learn about life which certainly is a learning opportunity.

There is an important need to provide in the curriculum ideas and activities to help the terminally ill student, a child with a disease which will eventually lead to death. The doctors and medical staff I had contact with, felt strongly that the terminally ill student should continue attending classes at school as long as possible.

The terminally ill student has many health concerns on his/her mind. But the child can get positive feedback and feel good about his/her achievement in school. Even if the terminally ill student is at home with a tutor, the classroom teacher and classmates can use some of the information in this book to help the terminally ill student forget about the disease. If this information can help the terminally ill student even for a brief time, then the goals for providing for individual needs will be accomplished.

The philosophy, goals and objectives of each individual school will determine how many activities or projects the classroom teacher can complete with the terminally ill student and the classmates. Also each classroom will be different because of the teaching styles, beliefs, creativity and strengths of each individual teacher.

The Wahpeton, North Dakota, Public School District allowed my second grade class to participate in the activities and events described in this book. This participation allowed a terminally ill student to believe and feel that he was an important member of our class even if he was at home or in the hospital.

The grade level of the children involved in this book was second grade; however, the ideas, activities and information can be adapted to any grade level. These activities will help not only the terminally ill student but also his/her classmates.

Educators will be able to use information from this book for helping students deal with the death of any loved one. Educators will also be able to use some of the ideas if there is a sudden accidental death of a classmate.

I've also written a book for primary-grade children called *Rainbows for Randy*. The objective of this children's book is to help a child deal with illness and death of a classmate or loved one.

Chapter 2

Information and Conferences with Parents, Doctors, Nurses, School Staff and Classmates

Schedule a conference as soon as school starts or whenever the teacher is made aware of the terminally ill student.

When talking to parents, remember they will show all sorts of emotions — anger, sadness, depression, etc. Parents want to talk about their child so be sure to ask about the child. Questions and suggestions on how to begin the conference are the responsibility of the teacher to help parents feel comfortable.

Ask parents for permission to use a tape recorder at the conference.

Taping the conference allows you to concentrate on visiting with the parents. Then you will have time to listen to the tape again and take notes. At this conference the educational goals for the terminally ill child should be determined for the school year.

With the parents consent, schedule another conference, to discuss the terminally ill student with support staff including other teachers, aides, administrative staff, cooks, janitor or any other person that would be in contact with the terminally ill student. An important role of the teacher at this time is to help the parents decide what information is to be given to school personnel.

The classroom teacher may need to get help from a support system outside of school, which might include: social workers, Hospice, doctors, nurses and the personnel at the child's treatment center.

At school the classroom teacher might receive support from the following: counselor, social worker, nurse and teachers who may have had experience with the death of a student. It is very emotional and overwhelming to have a terminally ill student in a classroom. From my personal experience, I found it extremely beneficial to receive support and strength from a support system. This support system will help the classroom teacher sort out feelings, provide courage and guidance, give advice, and be a sounding board for ideas during this difficult time.

Checklist of Questions to Ask Parents, Nurses and Doctors

- ☐ What is the disease?
- ☐ How is the disease being treated?
- ☐ Are there any pamphlets or materials available about this disease that the teacher can keep on file? This information will probably be read and re-read many times as the teacher looks for answers for many questions.
- ☐ Can the child attend school?
- ☐ How much time can the child attend school?
- ☐ Will medication be given at school? Be sure permission slip is signed so the teacher or nurse can legally give medication.
- ☐ What are the side effects of the disease and the side effects of medication that the teacher should be aware of in the classroom?
- ☐ In what school activities can this child participate?
- ☐ In what activities can this child not participate?
- ☐ Should this child be treated in any different ways from the other students? If so, how should this child be treated differently from the other students?

- ☐ How much does the terminally ill student know about the disease?
- ☐ How much should the classmates know about the terminally ill student?
- ☐ What does the future look like for this child?
- ☐ When does the child need to be absent from school for medical appointments, tests or treatments?
- ☐ Can the parents inform the teacher of changes in the child's condition as they occur?
- ☐ Could the nurses and doctors come to the classroom to help explain the disease to the classmates?
- ☐ Could the nurses and doctors continue to come to the classroom as the condition of the terminally ill student progresses?
- ☐ Could the teacher be involved with Hospice or other support groups to help the students?

Chapter 3

Ideas and Activities To Enhance Curriculum for Terminally Ill Students and Their Classmates

Stories

Have classmates tape record stories that the terminally ill student can listen to at home. These stories can be from the reading lesson or any library book. The students can take turns reading the story. Be sure to state the name of the reader before the story starts. The terminally ill student can follow along in his/her book or just listen to it for enjoyment. But most important the terminally ill student can hear the voices of his/her classmates.

Happy Pills

Our class collected empty Leggs Pantyhose containers which we called "happy pills." Each student took a "happy pill" home to fill with surprises. These surprise packages were filled with stickers, toy cars, toy farm machinery, small animals or erasers, and many things that excite a second grade boy. Each student was thrilled to share the surprises that he/she had put in the container. We taped the "happy pills" shut and lovingly decorated them. The news and excitement of our "happy pills" spread throughout our school. Soon more classes and staff members brought "happy pills" that they had filled for Randy.

Randy was able to stop at our room for a short visit before he left for his bone marrow transplant. We were so thrilled to give him our "happy pills." It was such a heart-warming experience to see the real meaning of giving to others. Each child carefully put his/her "happy pill" in a special schoolbag which was donated to Randy. We called these containers "happy pills" because Randy was to open one each day and try to forget about his sickness for awhile.

Film Containers

For Christmas, we filled empty 35 mm film containers with gifts of money. Each family decided how much money was to be put in each container. Then each container was wrapped with Christmas wrappings and put in a Christmas stocking for Randy. Randy was to use this to buy something for himself for Christmas. Other classes and staff members added containers filled with money to our stocking also.

Individual Class Pictures

We made a laminated poster with individual class pictures and printed names of each student under each picture. This poster was very beneficial with putting together names and faces when the terminally ill student received mail, talked on the phone or listened to the video tape recordings. This poster also reminded the sick child of all the friends who were thinking about him.

Happiness in Second Grade Is ...

For American Education Week, we made a poster that was displayed in the store window. The theme of the poster was Happiness in Second Grade. Our class made a page for Randy, which we hung in the store window too, that included our feelings. Happiness in any grade could be used.

Thumbprint Art

Press thumb in ink stamp pad. Each student designed pictures made of thumbprints. A fine line marker was used to add features to the pictures. Sometimes just thumb prints were added as a border around the letter for special designed stationery.

Bookmarks

For Book Week students designed and made special book markers. Each book mark was then laminated for Randy.

Stickers

Second graders love stickers. We used stickers in the following ways: stickers for individual letters, stickers for group letters, pages of stickers to give to the doctors and nurses, holiday stickers to hand out to visitors at the hospital, and stickers to put on the outside of each envelope mailed to Randy.

Art

Sometimes we sent art materials so Randy could make and complete the art activity at home or at the hospital. We also sent completed art activities which could be used to decorate his room.

Classroom Window

In our classroom window we put the letters, "Welcome Home Randy, We ♥ You."

We put this in the window after he came home from his bone marrow transplant. He loved to drive by the school and read the sign. Any words could be put on the windows and changed as often as the class wanted to change the letters.

Telephone

Each week we called Randy on the telephone. The students each took a turn talking to Randy. Some students wrote the things they wanted to tell Randy on paper. That way they could start talking immediately. Some students were able to talk to Randy without any notes. There was a telephone in the hall outside our classroom door. This telephone had a speaker on it, so each child could always hear what Randy was saying too.

Telegram

For Thanksgiving we went to Western Union. We prepared a telegram which was sent to Randy at the hospital, so we learned all about the uses of telegrams. Telegrams could be sent at any time of the year.

Videos

One of the parents came to school to make videos for special occasions, and we sent these videos to our friend. He would then send the tape back to us so we could add something new. We made a video for Halloween, Thanksgiving, Christmas, Valentine's Day, and when we visited Randy at the hospital.

Halloween

We made a video tape with the students in their Halloween costumes. Each child then took off his/her mask and talked to our classmate. We also used the video to show Randy our class carving jack-o-lanterns and making Witches' Brew.

Thanksgiving

We each designed a colorful letter in the "Happy Thanksgiving Randy" message. Each child wrote a note to Randy about that particular letter. We put these notes together and made a video. We also added to the video one of our Physical Education classes.

Christmas

We sang Christmas songs that we had learned for our program for a video tape. One of the TV stations came to our classroom to do a news story about the things we were doing for our classmate. We made a video while the TV crew was there filming. Our room was set up like a workshop with students doing the following activities for our classmate:

- ☐ writing a class letter,
- ☐ reading Christmas stories on the tape,
- ☐ coloring a computer banner,
- ☐ designing a poster "Merry Christmas, Randy" with red and green glitter,
- ☐ painting Christmas pictures,
- ☐ making Santa Christmas candy jar and wreath,
- ☐ wrapping 35 mm film containers with gifts of money inside.

Valentine's Day

Randy came to visit us for a short time so we made special Valentines for him. Each one of us read our card to him.

Class Letters

We taped a large piece of paper on the chalkboard. During the day each child added a sentence or two to the letter. When the letter was finished, it was decorated with pictures. This is an excellent activity because the students shared the activities of the classroom, and also were learning the parts of a friendly letter. Sometimes we each chose a favorite sticker to put on this letter.

Individual Letters

Each child wrote an individual letter on special paper. This paper had designs of a holiday, season, animal or anything that interested a second grader. I found that in the individual letters, the students shared their feelings more than they did with the class letters. The students shared how much they liked their sick classmate, how much they wanted the horrible disease to go away, and any of the classroom news.

Thank You Letters

We wrote and learned about thank you letters. We sent thank you letters for the following: when Randy made and sent us Halloween sucker ghosts, when Randy brought us Valentine cookies and red teddy bears, and when Randy had a pizza party for us.

Randy's parents shared with me how much they could see the other students improving with their writing skills because of the letters we sent during the year.

Addresses

Sending something in the mail each day was an excellent way to learn the correct form for writing addresses on envelopes.

Photographs

Pictures can be taken of the classroom and students doing different classroom activities. The terminally ill child probably is doing the same activity but at home alone with a tutor. This child identifies with his/her classmates when photographs show that either at school with the teacher or at home with a tutor, the same learning experiences are happening.

Computer

The computer can be used to make cards, pictures and banners. Each child takes a turn coloring a letter or a picture. It is real important to have each student sign his/her name. The second graders liked to do the banners the best. To them it seemed like we had made something really big because the banners were always so long and colorful. Here are some ideas for banners:

- ☐ Get Well Randy
- ☐ Merry Christmas Randy
- ☐ We Miss You Randy
- ☐ Kids Care for Randy
- ☐ Randy Is Home
- ☐ Happy Halloween
- ☐ Happy Easter
- ☐ Happy Birthday
- ☐ Have a Good Day
- ☐ Smile — We Love You

"Kids Care" Contest

As a result of the class interaction with Randy, our second grade class was the first place winner for second graders in the National Kids Care Contest, Scholastic News, New York. We made a video when our class went to the hospital to present him with his $1,000 check that we had won. He had a party for us, complete with pizza, cake, balloons and a special clown, Rainbow Love. It was a special time because we met his doctors and nurses. We were able to see his room decorated with our special things that we had made for him. This was the most special video because five days later our classmate died. We didn't know that our hugs and handshakes that day would be our last ones.

At the end of the school year I also made copies of these videos for any of the students who brought a video tape to school.

Special Papers and Journals

Keep special papers such as poetry, stories, thoughts and ideas of the terminally ill student in a file. If your class does writing in a journal, be sure to save the journal of the terminally ill student. These special keepsakes could be given to the family after the child has died.

Miscellaneous Activities

These activities could be done individually or in a group to help relieve stress before and after the death of a classmate:

- ☐ painting, cutting and pasting with arts and crafts,
- ☐ reading of poetry,
- ☐ role playing,
- ☐ puppetry, and
- ☐ many, many discussions.

Chapter 4

News of the Death of a Classmate

If the death occurs during the school day, it is very beneficial if the classroom teacher can spend a few minutes alone before the students are told. If it is possible for someone else to be in the classroom for a brief time, the teacher will be able to adjust somewhat before telling the class.

If the death doesn't occur during the school day, the classroom teacher will have time to think about the death before telling the class.

It is important to gather as many of the school staff as are available to help inform the classmates. Support can be received from the school psychologist, school counselor, school social worker, classroom teacher, administrative staff, school nurse or any available school staff person.

Some students will ask many questions. Some students will be quiet. Some students will cry. Some students will want to be alone. Some students will want to be held. There will probably be as many different reactions as there are students in the classroom. That is why it is very important to have other school staff available to help the classroom teacher when discussing the death of a classmate. The school staff can listen, hug, watch and hold any student that might need extra help. The students will show all kinds of emotions. From observations, the teacher will be able to decide what kind of comfort the students will need. Some students will probably act out their feelings instead of talking about them.

If possible, gather the students and school staff together in a semi-circle or as close together as possible. Everyone might also be sitting on the floor for closeness. Being together provides time for the students to grieve.

Instead of having the classroom teacher tell the students about the death of their classmate, it might be beneficial to involve the school counselor. During the discussion it is very important to use the words *died, dead* and *death*. The school counselor can answer these questions in the information given to the class:

- ☐ When did the classmate die?
- ☐ Why did the classmate die? (if the reason is known.)
- ☐ How did the classmate die? (if the reason is known.)
- ☐ Where did the classmate die?

The school counselor can discuss clearly and honestly the following information with the class:

- ☐ There is no right way to respond to death because we all have different feelings.
- ☐ Be sure to express your feelings to any caring adult.
- ☐ It is OK to cry.

- ☐ We all are sad in different ways and times.
- ☐ We all have different feelings of anger.
- ☐ Sadness and tears help us feel better later.
- ☐ We all aren't going to die now just because someone we love died.
- ☐ Our sadness can last for a long time.
- ☐ There is an empty feeling for that special person.
- ☐ No one can ever take away our special memories and times that we shared together.
- ☐ After our sadness we can laugh and talk about our happy times together.
- ☐ Dying is natural.
- ☐ Dying is the final part of everyone's life. The body has stopped working. The person will not become alive again. The person can't move, think, read or run again.
- ☐ Our special loved one always leaves something behind because we remember special things about that person.
- ☐ People who die will still be special to us.
- ☐ That special person will always live on forever in our hearts.

The students might ask some of the following questions and probably many more questions now or even later:

- ☐ Can my classmate still come to school?
- ☐ What is it like to die?
- ☐ Is my classmate sleeping?
- ☐ Does it hurt to die?
- ☐ Are all the hospital bills paid now?
- ☐ Did I help make my classmate die?

The students might ask these questions over and over to help develop strength and reassurance to deal with their fears of death. Be very supportive and acknowledge the feelings of the students.

The public school educators must remember there will be spiritual questions that need to be answered by parents at home. Questions about heaven, angels and the afterlife deal with the different religious beliefs of each family. It is important that the public school educator not teach his/her religious beliefs about death and dying to the students.

Families will have answers to the spiritual questions according to their religious beliefs. When a child asked, I told him/her that these religious questions should be answered by someone at home.

The students need to know that the teacher or other school staff are having a difficult time too. If the students see that the adults are sad, they will begin to understand that sadness is part of the grieving for their classmate who has died.

It would be very beneficial to tape record this discussion between the class and the professionals concerning the death of a classmate. After school, the support staff involved could have a conference and discuss the reactions of the students. This information could be recorded and kept on file. This information might be helpful later if a particular student is having an extremely difficult time dealing with the death of the classmate. It would also be easier for the classroom teacher to respond to parents if they ask how their child responded to the news. In the future the classroom teacher should also record any information which might mean a particular child is having difficulty dealing with the death. This information should also be available to the principal in case the child needs extra help from support services at a later time.

The administration should send a note home with each child explaining that a classmate has died. This note could also explain how this information was shared with the class. The parents could also be given the telephone number of the counselor or teacher if more help or information is needed. It is important to stress to the parents that any unusual behaviors should be shared with the classroom teacher.

Chapter 5

Preparing For the Funeral

A. Before the Funeral

A note should be sent home from the administration concerning the funeral. The note should include when and where the funeral will be held. The note should also explain whether or not the students will be going to the funeral as a class, if the class is riding on the school bus or walking, if the students will be meeting at the church, or if each student should attend the funeral with his/her family. Be sure there is a permission note to sign if the student can attend the funeral with the class. It is very important to have the students help with the planning of preparations. It is also important to keep the students informed of the activities of the funeral that will take place.

Discussions

Discuss the following questions and information with the students before the funeral:

- ☐ When will the funeral be?
- ☐ Where will the funeral be?
- ☐ What will the church or room look like? (The teacher might visit this place before to explain to the students the details.)
- ☐ What will the students hear?
- ☐ Where will the dead person be?

- ☐ What will be the people be doing? Be sure to mention that they will see many people crying, talking and hugging.
- ☐ What is the church service like and what will happen during the church service?
- ☐ What will the dead person be wearing? (Ask the funeral director.)
- ☐ Why are there many flowers at a funeral?
- ☐ Will our class send flowers?
- ☐ Will our class go together on a school bus or walk? Or will the class meet together if the funeral is not during the regular school day?
- ☐ Can parents come along or meet us at the funeral?
- ☐ What is a casket? Be sure to explain that a casket is a box that the dead person will be placed in.
- ☐ What are casket bearers? They are special people chosen by the family to carry the casket. Our class was chosen to be honorary casket bearers. As honorary casket bearers, our class walked down the church aisle together before the casket. We sat on the steps of the altar during the funeral.

Receiving the news of the death of a classmate is a very tense and difficult time for the students. It is very important to take time during the school day to meet the needs of the students. I found it necessary to do many different activities to help each child deal with his/her own steps of grieving which includes: denial, anger, bargaining, depression and finally acceptance. These stages of grieving are taken from Elizabeth Kubler Ross's book *On Death and Dying*.

After the funeral it was then easier to settle down to the regular routine of the school day. It is important for educators to remember that education is all about preparing students for life. What better way to prepare students for life than to include some of the following activities rather than sticking to the teachers manual during this difficult time? You will indeed find out that these activities pertain to different areas of the curriculum.

Classroom Activities

Pictures

Students can draw or paint a picture of what they think death might look like. Students can write or talk about what dying might feel like. The class could make a group book of thoughts and pictures of experiences they had concerning death.

Chalkboard

The class can develop on the chalkboard topics about death. Some topics to develop and discuss or write about could be:

Death Is:
What Is Dead?
My First Experience With Death

Poem

The class could write a group poem or class story about their dead classmate, or the class could just write simple sentences about their classmate. These sentences could be put together as one poem or story. The classroom teacher could ask the family if this poem or story could be read by a classmate at the funeral.

Library Books

Ask the librarian to check out all the children's book on death and dying. Use these books to read to the class during this difficult time. Have the books available on a shelf in the classroom. Then anytime during the day the students will feel free to browse or read these books again for strength or reassurance.

Ask the librarian for a list of books available for parents to read. These books could help parents deal with the steps of grieving with their children at home. I also use these books to send home with a child when he/she experiences the loss of any loved one. When a parent reads these children's books with his/her child, it is easier for the parents to discuss the death with a child.

There is a list of resource books on death and dying in Chapter 7 of this book.

Casket Pictures

A picture, note or drawing can be placed in the casket. This might include feelings for the classmate that has died or something special about the classmate. Be sure to check with the funeral director so these notes are placed in the casket at the appropriate time.

Feelings

It is excellent therapy to have the classmates write about the feelings of the death of their classmate. These could be shared with the classroom teacher or the family of the classmate who has died, or else just kept private.

Doctors and Nurses

The doctor or nurse of the classmate who has died could return to the class to explain to the students why the classmate has died. These people could answer any questions the students might ask.

Funeral Directors

First you should interview the funeral director to determine if a visit with the director would be beneficial to the class. Funeral directors could come to the classroom to discuss and answer questions. The funeral director could share videos or books that he/she has on file. It is the responsibility of the teacher to preview this material before it is shared with the class.

Memorial or Flowers

If school policy allows, and if you decide the class should send a memorial, then the class should discuss and decide what would be appropriate. Be sure to discuss that a memorial is something special given by the class in memory of their classmate who has died.

One idea that our class used was for each child to pick his/her favorite color. The floral shop then dyed carnations in each child's favorite color. Each child carried his/her favorite colored carnation and placed it in a special vase at the beginning of the funeral.

Our special rainbow-colored carnations were the most beautiful flowers at the funeral because we knew that Randy loved rainbows. It would really be special if after the funeral, the flowers would be sent back to the school. For art class, each carnation could be pressed and glued on a card so each child could have a special keepsake.

Our class also ordered an engraved plaque and had it arranged in a blue floral arrangement for Randy's family. The plaque read:

In Memory of Randy
Because Kids Care
Love
Mrs. Berg's Second Grade Class
1987–88

There are many ideas that could be used for memorials. Remember to think about the interests of the deceased classmate and the memorials will have extra special meaning to the remaining classmates.

Any of these memorials could be used: children's books for school or public library; tree, shrub or flowers planted in school yard; gift of money donated to family or special organization that was helpful to classmate that died; plaque for school; or anything special for the school. Brainstorm with the classmates and list all of their ideas on the chalkboard. Then have the classmates decide on the special memorial.

B. At the Funeral

At the funeral, the person in charge of the service will tell special things about the dead person. The students will be able to see that a funeral gives people a time and place to feel their sadness or grief. The students will be able to view the dead body of the classmate if they wish.

They will see that other people loved their classmate and will miss their classmate too.

The students will see that the people at the funeral get support from each other.

The students will see that people come to the funeral to talk to the family.

Students can now see that a funeral is a time to say goodby because the classmate is really dead.

Students won't always know what to do or say but will see that it is OK to cry at the funeral.

Attending the funeral is important because it helps the students to deal with death, to feel sad, and to share their feelings.

The students experienced sorrow, but were able to accept the pain and can remember the joy they experienced knowing that their love and caring made Randy's life brighter.

C. At the Cemetery

Some churches have committal services either at the church or at the cemetery. The classroom teacher needs to check before the funeral where the committal service will be held. Our class rode the school bus from the church to the cemetery in the country.

The students will see that the casket will be taken to the cemetery.

The students will see that the casket will be placed above the ground.

There will be a short prayer, reading and probably a song.

The children will see that a cemetery is a place where the casket is placed in the ground. Tell the children that after the people leave the cemetery, the casket will be lowered into a hole in the ground, then covered with soil. Grass and flowers will soon grow over the soil where the casket was placed. Later headstones, markers or monuments are engraved and placed at the cemetery. The name of the classmate, his birthday, his date of death, his picture and a special verse are engraved on the monument.

Each student held a blue balloon at the cemetery. When the short service was over at the cemetery, each second grader released his balloon into the sky; releasing the balloons helped the second graders understand that this was like letting go of the special classmate.

A flower or flowers could also be placed on the casket.

D. After the Cemetery

We rode the school bus from the cemetery back to the church.

Our class sat together for lunch at the church. During this time, everyone was a typical second grader. It was a special time to be together eating, laughing, visiting and talking after experiencing the funeral of a very special friend who will never be forgotten.

After lunch we shared hugs and goodbys with Randy's family.

We rode the school bus back to our school. It was a typical bus ride with noisy, excited second graders.

The death of our special classmate was a difficult concept to try to comprehend. It certainly was a tremendous learning experience for the children and also for me. Because of this experience, these second graders will be able to find support for other difficult situations in their life.

Chapter 6

Life Goes On

From my personal experiences and readings, I feel it is so very important that educators first accept their own beliefs and feelings about death before they can truly help the students deal with their feelings and concerns about death!

The following quote was taken from Prophet Khalil Gibran: "Learning about death is actually at the same time learning about life." After experiencing the death and dying of a classmate, the students did learn so very much about life. After the funeral it is so important to realize that life does go on and on. We will never forget this person because of all our special memories.

Help the students discuss and realize that life will always change but yet continue, so it is important to carry on with the usual everyday school activities.

Discuss with the students the feelings they experienced during the funeral. It is important that the classroom teacher remembers to share his/her feelings, too. The students need to know that this experience was a difficult time for you too.

Discuss with the students that it is OK to cry, feel sorry, get mad or angry, and even get scared. No matter how we feel now, after a time we will feel better.

Remind the students to talk about death and their fears with the classroom teacher, their family members and other classmates. Sometimes it might be better for the students to talk with their classmates, who have shared the same experiences, rather than to talk with other adults. The students need not to feel alone or afraid because they can discuss their feelings and receive help and strength from the other classmates.

Remember that drawing, painting, writing and sharing activities release many different feelings.

The students might share what their families and classmates have done to help them through this sad time.

The students need lots of love, support and information from school and home.

It will be difficult to take the name off the student's desk. As time goes on it will be easier to look at the desk, photos or even talk about the special classmate.

On Randy's eighth birthday, we sent notes to Randy's family. We wanted the family to know that we were thinking about Randy and his family too.

For Mother's Day we planted extra marigold seeds. We wanted Randy's mother to have flowers from our class. Some of these special flowers were planted at the cemetery for Memorial Day.

We sent copies of the following special poem to Randy to give to his doctors and nurses. Randy had this poem taped to a wall at the hospital. It was then printed on his memorial program for his funeral.

Its message states that life does go on because of the special things that we do for each other.

A hundred years from now
it will not matter
what my bank account was,
the sort of house I lived in,
or the kind of clothes I wore.
But the world may be
much different
because I was important
in the life of a child.
— Author Unknown

Chapter 7

Resources for Teachers and Parents

Books for Children About People Dying

Aliki. *The Two of Them*. Greenwillow Books, 1979.

Buscaglia, Leo. *The Fall of Freddie the Leaf.* Holt, Rinehart, & Winston, 1982.

DePaola, Tomie. *Nana Upstairs & Nana Downstairs*. Putnam, 1973.

Fassler, Joan. *My Grandpa Died Today*. Behavioral Pub., Inc., New York, 1971.

Miles, Miska. *Annie and the Old One*. Little, Brown & Co., 1971.

Peavy, Linda. *Allison's Grandfather*. Charles Scribner's Sons., New York, 1981.

Smith, Doris Buchanan. *A Taste of Blackberries*. Thomas Y. Crowell Co., 1973.

Stein, Sara. *About Dying: An Open Family Book for Parents and Children Together*. Walker & Co., 1974.

Zolotow, Charlotte. *My Grandson Lew*. Harper & Tow, 1974.

Books for Children About Pets Dying

Adams, Adrienne. *The Wounded Duck*. Charles Scribner's Sons, New York. 1979.

Brown, Margaret Wise. *The Dead Bird*. Addison-Wesley, 1983.

Carrick, Carol. *The Accident*. Houghton-Mifflin, 1976.

Conen, Miriam. *Jim's Dog Muffins*. Willow Books, 1984.

Hurd, Edith Thachner. *The Black Dog Who Went Into the Woods*. Harper and Row Pub., 1980.

Mellonie, Bruan. *Lifetimes: the Beautiful Way to Explain Death to Children*. Bantam, 1983.

Otsuka, Yuzo. *Suko and the White Horse*. Viking, 1981.

Stevens, Carla. *Stories from a Snowy Meadow*. Seabury Press, 1976.

Varley, Susan. *Badger's Parting Gift*. Lothrop, Lee & Shepard, 1984.

Viorst, Judith. *The Tenth Good Thing About Barney*. Atheneum, 1981.

Wilhelm, Hans. *"I'll Always Love You." Crown, 1985.*

Williams, Margery. *The Velveteen Rabbit*. Avon Books. 1975.

Thanks so much to everyone who remembered us in their thoughts during this difficult time. Thanks, too, for always being there for me — Dave, Amy and Shawn; Wilfred Sauer; all of my family; the Wahpeton, North Dakota, school staff; and the people of Wahpeton and the surrounding communities.

About the Author

Julie Berg has taught primary school for more than 26 years, the last 21 of them as a second grade teacher in Wahpeton, North Dakota. A native of Great Bend, North Dakota, and graduate of Moorhead (Minnesota) State University, she wrote this book and a companion for children, *Rainbows for Randy,* under North Dakota's 1989 Christa McAuliffe Fellowship. Her class received first place in Scholastic News' 1987–1988 "Kids Care" Contest; Mrs. Berg has also been honored as U.S. West Outstanding Teacher for North Dakota and the Jaycees' Outstanding Educator of the Year. She and her husband Dave have two children, Amy and Shawn.

About the Illustrator

Kimberly K. Gwynn, an elementary teacher, is Julie Berg's niece. She lives in Eagle River, Alaska.